Contents

Some words are shown in bold, **like this**. You can find them in the glossary on page 23.

What is swimming?

Swimming is exercise we do in water. You can swim in the sea or in a swimming pool.

Some people swim in competitions and races. Other people just swim to keep fit and have fun.

How do I learn to swim?

You need an adult to teach you how to swim. A teacher at your school or a swimming teacher could teach you at a swimming pool.

To start you need to get used to
putting your face in the water. You
might use **floats** to help you learn
to swim.

How do I use my arms?

You use your arms to pull yourself through the water. You can move your arms in different ways, called **strokes**.

You can use your arms to push down on the side of the pool so you can climb out.

How do I use my legs?

You use your legs to kick. This helps you to move through the water. When you kick hard, you swim faster.

You use your legs when you jump or dive into the pool. You should bend your knees before you jump.

How do I use the rest of my body?

You can **float** on your back near the top of the water.

You learn how to hold your breath and open your eyes under water. You move your head up or to the side to breathe when you swim.

What happens to my body when I swim?

When you get into the pool the water might make you feel colder. As you swim you will feel warmer and you will breathe faster.

muscle

Your heart will start to beat faster.
The **muscles** in your arms and legs
will feel tired.

How does it feel to swim?

Swimming is a good way to have fun. You might make new friends as you swim together.

It feels good to get better at swimming. When you swim further or faster you might get a special badge or medal.

How do I stay safe swimming?

Always listen to your teacher or the **lifeguard**. Make sure you know the rules at the swimming pool.

Never run by the pool because you could slip. When you jump into the pool check nobody is in the way and that the water is deep enough.

Does swimming make me healthy?

Swimming is good exercise and will help to keep you fit. To stay healthy you also need to get plenty of rest.

You should also eat healthy food every day and drink plenty of water.

Swimming equipment

goggles

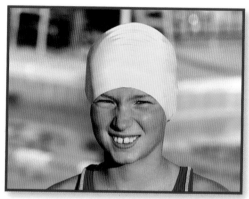

swimming cap

towel

Glossary

 **float** stay near the top of water

 **floats** things that float in water and can be used to help people learn to swim

 **lifeguard** someone who works at a swimming pool or on a beach, who helps people to stay safe in the water

 **muscle** part of your body that helps you to move. Exercise can make muscles bigger and stronger.

 **stroke** in swimming a stroke is a movement you make with your arms or legs to help you move through the water

Index

Find out more

http://kidshealth.org/kid/watch/out/water.html
Find out how to stay safe in and around water.

http://www.videojug.com/film/basic-swimming-strokes-for-young-children-5-7-years-2
This website includes some basic swimming strokes to help you practise.